My State KANSAS

By Christina Earley

TABLE OF CONTENTS

A Crabtree Seedlings Book

Crabtree Publishing

crabtreebooks.com

School-to-Home Support for Caregivers and Teachers

This book helps children grow by letting them practice reading. Here are a few guiding questions to help the reader build his or her comprehension skills. Possible answers appear in red.

Before Reading:

- What do I know about Kansas?
    - *I know that Kansas is a state.*
    - *I know that there are bison in Kansas.*

- What do I want to learn about Kansas?
    - *I want to learn which famous people were born in Kansas.*
    - *I want to learn what the state flag looks like.*

During Reading:

- What have I learned so far?
    - *I have learned that Topeka is the state capital of Kansas.*
    - *I have learned that there are more than 4,000 species of plants at the Botanica Gardens in Wichita.*

- I wonder why...
    - *I wonder why the state flower is the wild sunflower.*
    - *I wonder why there are so many bison at the Maxwell Wildlife Refuge.*

After Reading:

- What did I learn about Kansas?
    - *I have learned that Wichita is the largest city in Kansas.*
    - *I have learned that the state animal is the buffalo.*

- Read the book again and look for the glossary words.
    - *I see the word **capital** on page 6, and the word **refuge** on page 16. The other glossary words are found on pages 22 and 23.*

KANSAS

I live in Olathe. My city's name comes from the Shawnee Native American word for "beautiful."

My city is known for making cowboy boots.

Kansas is in the **midwestern** United States. The **capital** is Topeka.

Fun Fact: Wichita is the largest city in Kansas.

The state animal is the American buffalo.

The wild sunflower is the state flower.

We grow a lot of wheat in Kansas. Some of it is used to make bread.

Fun Fact: Kansas is one of the states that **produces** the most wheat in the U.S.

My state flag is blue. The state **seal** is in the middle.

The city of Lebanon is in the center of the United States.

I like to go to Botanica Gardens in Wichita. There are more than 30 different gardens.

Fun Fact: There are more than 4,000 species of plants at the gardens.

The Maxwell Wildlife **Refuge** has the state's largest herd of **bison**.

I have fun with my family at Kansas Speedway.

Pilot Amelia Earhart was born in Kansas. Gale Sayers, who was an NFL running back, was also born in Kansas.

Fun Fact: Former senator Bob Dole was born in Russell, Kansas.

My family likes to visit Strataca, the underground salt museum. We take an elevator that goes deep underground to the museum.

At Rock City I like to climb on the huge rocks. Some of them are as big as a house!

Glossary

bison (bie-sin): A large, hairy wild animal that has horns

capital (cap-ih-tuhl): The city or town where the government of a country, state, or province is located

midwestern (mid-west-urn): The northern central part of the United States

produces (pruh-doos-es): Makes or grows something for sale or use

refuge (ref-yooj): An area where animals and plants are protected

seal (seel): A special design that is used on important papers and other items

Index

About the Author

Christina Earley lives in sunny South Florida with her husband and son. She enjoys traveling around the United States and learning about different historical places. Her hobbies include hiking, yoga, and baking.

Written by: Christina Earley
Designed and Illustrated by: Bobbie Houser
Series Development: James Earley
Proofreader: Melissa Boyce
Educational Consultant: Marie Lemke M.Ed.

Photographs:
Alamy: Everett Collection Inc: p. 18 right; Philip Scalia: p. 21
LOC: p. 19
Shutterstock: Rachael Martin: cover; Jeff Kuhlman: p. 3; PhotoTrippingAmerica: p. 4; IrynaN: p. 5; Volina: p. 6, 22; Sean Pavone: p. 7; O.S. Fisher: p. 8; Elizabeth May Photography: p. 9; Charles Lemar Brown: p. 10-11; Scorpp: p. 11, 23; railway fx: p. 12, 23; Lost_in_the_Midwest: p. 13; Gary L. Brewer: p. 14-15; Danita Delimont: p. 15; Ricardo Reitmeyer: p. 16, 22-23; Grindstone Media Group: p. 17; Everett Collection: p. 18 left; Robert D Brozek: p. 20

Crabtree Publishing

crabtreebooks.com 800-387-7650

Printed in the U.S.A./072023/CG20230214

Published in Canada
Crabtree Publishing
616 Welland Avenue
St. Catharines, Ontario
L2M 5V6

Published in the United States
Crabtree Publishing
347 Fifth Avenue
Suite 1402-145
New York, New York, 10016

Library and Archives Canada Cataloguing in Publication
Available at Library and Archives Canada

Library of Congress Cataloging-in-Publication Data
Available at the Library of Congress

Hardcover: 978-1-0398-0515-6
Paperback: 978-1-0398-0547-7
Ebook (pdf): 978-1-0398-0611-5
Epub: 978-1-0398-0579-8